A gift for
Sharon Patterson

Rhonda

from

2002

Copyright © 2000 by Joy Marie Heimsoth

Published under license from J. Countryman®
a division of Thomas Nelson, Inc.

Project Editor – Terri Gibbs

All rights reserved.
No portion of this publication may be reproduced,
stored in a retrieval system or transmitted in any form by
any means - electronic, mechanical, photocopying, recording,
or any other - except for brief quotations in printed
reviews, without the prior written permission of the publisher.

Designed by Starletta Polster, Murfreesboro, Tennessee

ISBN: 0-8499-9616-3 (Hallmark Edition)

www.jcountryman.com
www.hallmark.com

Printed in China

I celebrate you

One of the things I appreciate most about you, Mom, is

_____

_____

_____

_____

_____

I celebrate your STRENGTH

A mother like you makes all the difference.

This is one way you have made a difference in my life~

_____

_____

_____

_____

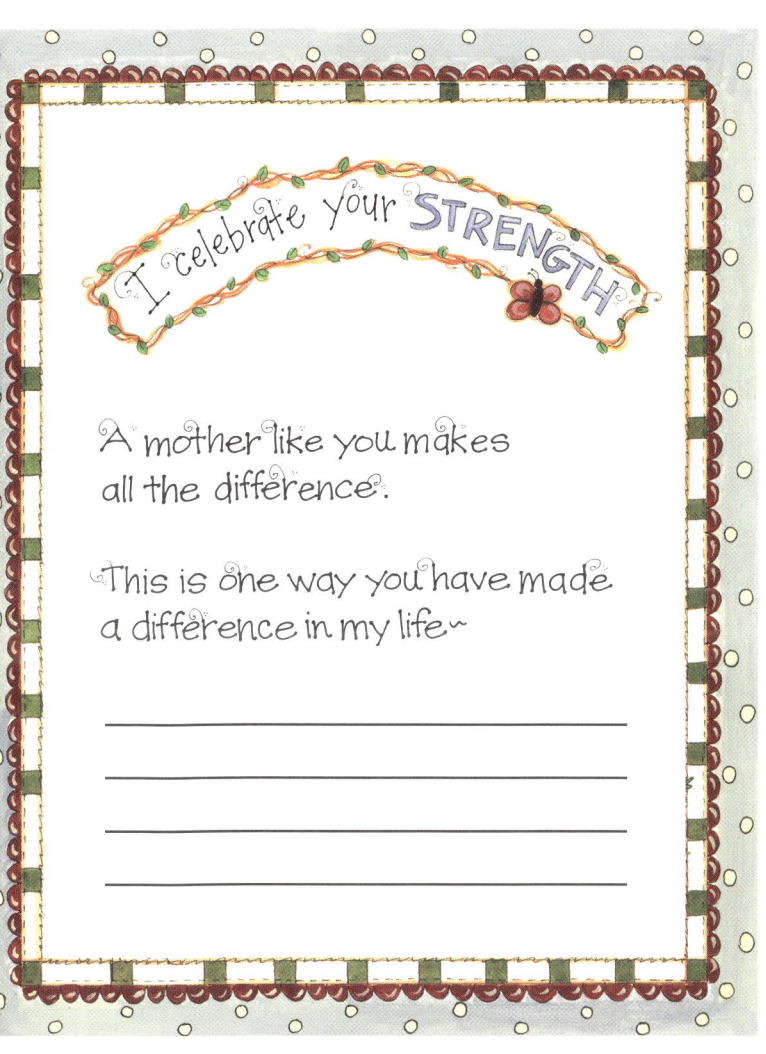

I celebrate your UNDERSTANDING

Mom,
You always know how to make my heart smile.

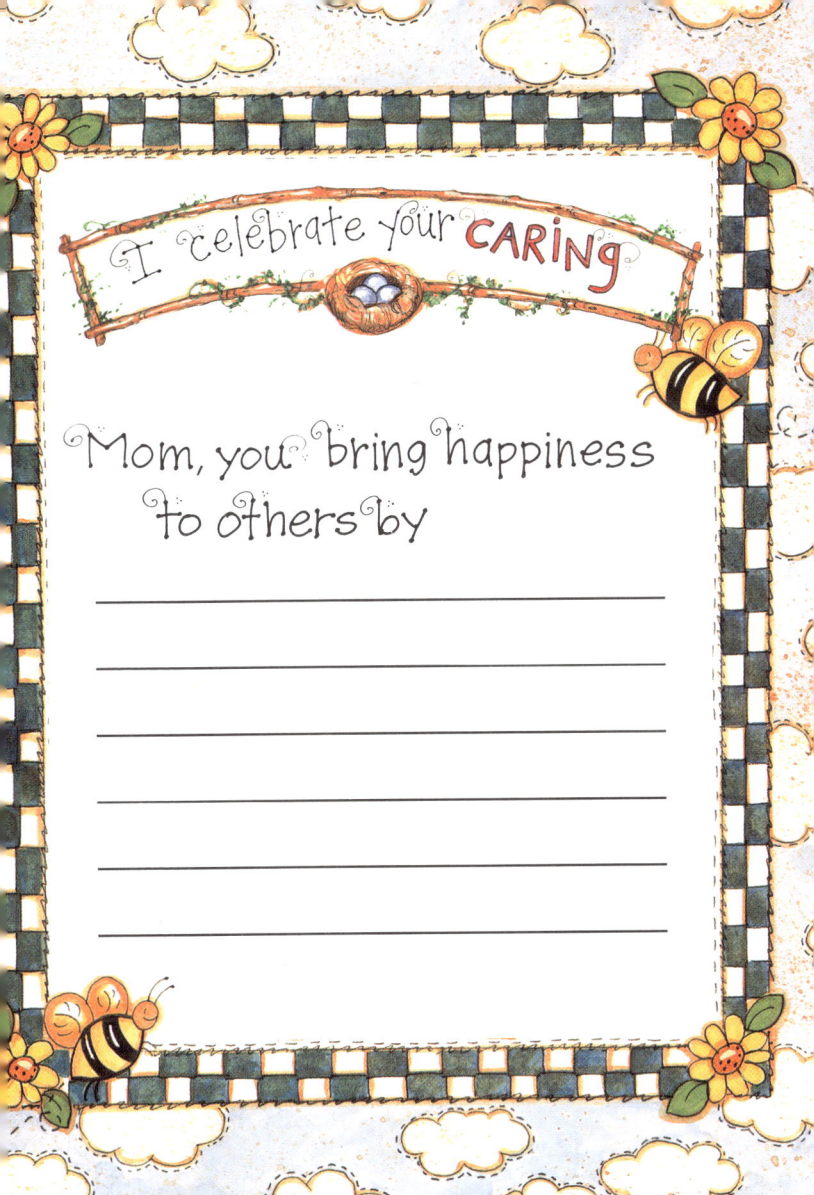

I celebrate your Encouragement

With poems, praise and
promises to share
a mother's love
will always be there.

This is my wish for you, Mom:

_____

_____

_____

_____

_____

_____

_____

A mother's tender, warm embrace

is a special gift of care and grace.